UNREQUITED LOVE

LOVE OR SELF RESPECT

ADITYA PRATAP SINGH

Copyright © Aditya Pratap Singh
All Rights Reserved.

This book has been published with all efforts taken to make the material error-free after the consent of the author. However, the author and the publisher do not assume and hereby disclaim any liability to any party for any loss, damage, or disruption caused by errors or omissions, whether such errors or omissions result from negligence, accident, or any other cause.

While every effort has been made to avoid any mistake or omission, this publication is being sold on the condition and understanding that neither the author nor the publishers or printers would be liable in any manner to any person by reason of any mistake or omission in this publication or for any action taken or omitted to be taken or advice rendered or accepted on the basis of this work. For any defect in printing or binding the publishers will be liable only to replace the defective copy by another copy of this work then available.

This is dedicated to everyone who had a crush in past or in present. It's a beautiful feeling. Maturity is when you understand life doesn't stop for anyone.

50% of the profit made through this book will be donated to army and underprevileged children.

Contents

Acknowledgements

I would like to express my deepest gratitude to Late. N.K Singh (My Grandpa) and will always be alive in my heart. I also owe a very important debt to My Friends they helped me in tough times whose meticulous comments were an enormous help to me. I would also like to express my gratitude to my family for their moral support and warm encouragements. Finally, I would like to express my gratitude to Reader for their financial support.

Prologue

This story is not a fictional story. It's the life experience of the author. Name of the boy and the girl is changed. Name of the cities are also different. This is the world's shortest novel. Kindly send a review at howtodo3192@gmail.com.

First Part

Hello, my self Aditya the author of this book this incident happens with me when I Just passed my class 10th board exam . Till class 10th I was an introvert by the way today also I am introvert but not that much.

Having a crush change you a lot .

I belong from a small town in Uttar Pradesh. I have a younger sibling brother. This story happens when I was in class 11th. My father's best friend daughter who is around 4 to 5 months younger than me. My father used to go to meet his best friend almost everyday because they both are childhood friends. As he was my father's close friend but because he had a dark past he spent almost 10 years in jail.

That girl name is Radhika she had completed class 10th from Varanasi. When her father got bail they maked there house and shifted in there hometown. We both have same hometown .

I wanted to change my school since my old school have some rules which I don't like rakhi (sacred thread) is not allowed. Since my school is so called secular.

I wanted to move to town for prepartion of IIT JEE. Since I am an aspirant its the other story. At that time I am giving the test of different - different institutes. I have got selection in many institutes for the preparation of engineering exams but the destiny had another plans for me.

A teacher of Jaipur who is one of my relative's from my aunt's (Mami) side. He is a teacher in a well known institute from Rajasthan (India). I have planned to move to Jaipur since that teacher lives in Jaipur.

All the plans were set we have decided to take admission in Jaipur school because my coaching will be done there in care of my guradian who is a teacher in that institute he too is from Ghazipur but shifted in Jaipur. My grandfather is sad because I am going far away from them. I was 16 that time.

I have never lived away from my grandfather because we have a joint family. My grandfather loves me a lot. He had done almost everything to convience and stop me because he wanted that I finish my schooling from my hometown because he don't want me that I go anywhere. Each time I asked him he said "Son don't worry of colleges I am always there for you. After 12th if you want to prepare then take a drop."

Deep down I know he was sad when he heard I was going. I have stucked between three things. I don't want to make him sad nor I wanted to miss my freedom because till class 10th I haven't gone out of the house but now I wanted to enjoy my freedom and focus on my career.

But here is the twist corona came and everything got closed 5 cases found in Jaipur. Meanwhile my grandfather was very happy. My online classes started and my schedule became hectic and my life became hell. I tooked 1 months classes then I know this thing is not my cup of my tea since there is a lockdown. There is a large difference between class 10th (Physics Chemistry Math) and class 12th (Physics Chemistry Math). I dropped my plan of going to Jaipur because of the pandemic and buyed a online course to help me.

Everthing got changed now I have to take admission in my hometown. I am searching for the school where to take admission she is also searching for the school. Later on while I am searching for my school I have seen many schools and getting opinions from parents. My granpa said to study me from the same school where I am studying from 12 years. But I got cemented on my decision to change my school. So he doesn't force me. My parents suggested me two school one school was of my father's junior (S Public School) and one was M Public School.

These were one of the top schools in the city. I decided to go to M Public School and she decided to go to S School. That time I don't know her nor she knows me. I tooked science side and she took commerce.

Everthing was going well. Online exams were to occur so I passed by cheating. The truth was that almost 99% of the people don't study during lockdown. Schools were closed online classes were running attendance is compulsory. Our school have it's own application where online classes were running.

So, I worked hard not to study, but to find bug in app. I got success and find a bug now I open app and make the attendance of the whole week just by changing the time. Days were passing but one day a news come offline exams will be held for class 11. After hearing this news most of the student got panic and later started for finding the solution. Except one student noone had studied anything. Exams were just 2 days far. So we studied only few topics just to pass the exam. Since no one had studied so teacher gave grace marks and passed everyone.

I passed class 11th . Corona was in peak at that time its the time of April 2021. My grandfather got illed. He was suffering from respiratory issues. There is a shortage of oxygen cylinder in all over India. We are feeling like helpless but my grandpa was brave. He doesn't tells his problem because he had very strength to endure.

One night his health got worsened. My father and uncle planned to take him to the Varanasi. Minutes are passing like year. That night nobody sleep well . I got sleep at around 2 AM. 22 April 2021 : Grandpa wake up at 4 AM and arouse Grandma to make tea. It's because he loves Tea which were made by Grandma especially morning. They both drinked tea together and then done little bit of breakfast. Then everybody left for varanasi. Varanasi was almost 70 km from Ghazipur.

It was around 9:45 AM or 10:00 AM . My mother (in a deep sad voice) - Wake Up Son Grandpa is no more ("Beta Utho Baba Nhi Rhe"). That word stops my mind all the dreams which were coming into my mind got stopped. It feel likes the whole world had stopped.

No thoughts ! all the time and the memories which we spent together just flash with rapid speed. No reaction on my face. I thought it was a bad dream. But later on I heared sound of crying. I washed my face. Its like the whole world had endup. He always say "until I will see your marriage nothing will happen to me". But he was a lier. He left us alone.

When they reached Varanasi infront of a BHU his oxygen level became zero. Neither my dad nor my uncle know what happened to him. He is talking with them and frequently asking questions like have we reached ? how much time ? Is Rupesh coming? (Rupesh is my middle uncle)

But suddenly everything happened in such a hurry at that time both of them brain became blank. They are also not from medical background so they don't know whats the meaning of zero oxygen. They refreshed the machine but it continuously showing zero. So they thought the machine got damaged and carried granpa in his arms when they reached infront of doctor. Doctor checked his nerves and declared him dead. One fact is that he studies agriculture from BHU and he left at the same campus.

Second Part

Her name is Radhika. A cool, awesome and traditional girl by whom everyone will fall in love with like others I will say too , she is differenet. Maybe my feeling for her made her different.

Her father is a businessman and mother is a housewife. She has a younger sister.

There is a festival when I have seen her photo on my mother phone. Her mother put onto her Whatsapp status. She is looking adorable in a traditional outfit. In my past I have seen many girls in my class but, I haven't talked with any of them nor has feeling for any of her. Instead of it I am the supporter of Masculism and the leader of boys of my class.

Before starting let me tell about mascuiism because some of you will think other thing especially feminist. I always supports boys but that doesn't means I suppress girls. I respect them a lot but some girls tries to use their girl power just to suppress boys. I am the staunch opponent of those girls and this mentality. Even had done fights for the boys and the result I have all male friends and don't talk to any girl because they had different groups. So till then my girls interaction ratio is zero.

A fine day she along with her family were invited to my house for dinner. When I have her first seen her I feel like an angel had comed to our house. I got nervous by looking her because she is beautiful. I am an introvert so i quickly went into my room and phoned a random friend and started talking with him. They were sitting on nearby room my voice is going into the room may be.

Her mother asked by mother to give a tour of our house. She along with mother were having a tour after sometimes she came into my room.

She - Is this your elder son?

Mom- Yes

I am talking with my friend and wearing a headset and my backportion was infront of the door. I sees her in the mirror. I went quickly and touched her feet. She blessed me and gives me compliment.

Time is passing l have fear that it's not good if they leave without meeting me. It's not good for me not for them because I wanted to meet her. Hahahaha Then after some time my mother called me.

Mom- Adi come here ?

Me - Ok Just 2 minutes

Deep down I am happy and nevous at the same time. I don't know what to say how to behave and talk. My heart started beating fast. I drank water and stayed in my room. Then my father called me.

Father - It's been around 5 minutes come here

Me - Ok

I am thinking of a new idea to postpone this because each second my nervousness was increasing.

Then after sometimes my mother came in my room..

Mom- Aren't you listening we are calling you?

Me - Umm But i have some work

Mom - Just go and meet them sit for five minutes with them after that come back to the room.

Me - Ok

Mom - Come with me

i followed her and enters the room. I sees her

at that time I guess she had weard jeans and shirt. I don't remeber her dress because looking into her eyes was like a man in front of ocean I got lost. Then her father puts her hand on my shoulder. I thought I gonna be beaten hard. He is sitting with me. I touched his feet.

Uncle - God bless you.Then said to my father your child had grown up.

I am the center of attraction everyone is looking towards me. Everyone is asking me question.

Uncle - You are in which class?

Me - 12th Science side

Uncle - Meet my daughter. Her name is Lori she too is in class 12 from commerce side

She looked on my eyes it was the first eye contact with her. I said nice.

Uncle : How is my daughter.

After this I got blushed like hell and a smile came into my face.

May be her mother read my face.

Aunty to uncle - Leave it naa may be he has work let him finish his work first.

After that I came into my room. 5 minutes passed I wanted to see her again and praying to god that anyone please call me. This time I will not take even a single second. But sadly no-one called me after 2 minutes I looked towards my water bottle it was empty. I had a plan. I take the water bottle and went towards the kitchen the room in which she were sitting was on the way. I sees her again and filled my bottle.

I repeated this thing many times at the gap of couple of minutes. Each time I fill water bottle then go to washroom or garden and empty the water bottle. This process repeats many times. Lastly when I goes to fill the water bottle her mother along with my mother were present in the kitchen. Again I guess she read my face.

i aborted this plan because if I repeat this in front of them then I will be caught. I am thinking of the new plan. Her younger sister came into my room. She is in 2nd she came and said to me "What's your name ? "I am talking with her. Some of her words were not clear to me. Then after some time she went back. I sensed anyone is standing on the door. But avoided it and started listening music on high volume.

After some time i got confirmed because i have seen a shadow but by then it was too late. That shadow went smaller and smaller. I chased that shadow and followed it but found no one.

Mom called me for dinner but it was too early and I got a important call so I said I will eat later. When they were leaving my father called me again to say goodbye.

When I was having dinner.

Mom - What have you talked?

Me - With Whom?

Mom - That girl.

Me - I was sitting in front of you have you seen me talking with her.

Mom - I am not asking about that I am asking when she goes to meet you in your room what have talked with her.

Me- When she had come into my room. I don't know what are you saying.

She - You both were together for 30 minutes.

Me (lied)- She was sitting on sofa and I am completing my work.

I asked " Why she came into my room".

Mom - Because her mother had said her to go into your room.

i missed an opportunity to talk to her. After some day new year came there is a party at night we went into her house. Only fathers friends and there family's are allowed. Ladies are into another room. Gents are into different and children are into different. There are totally 8 peop;e (child) including me present in that room. There is a person who is 2-3 years senior than me he studies in Chennai. First 1 hour I just behave like I am busy in my phone. But the main problem is there is no internet connection on that room. I tried my father mother phone too but internet connection was not present.

I am getting bored then my father introduces me and my senior. Then i asked many questions. We have a healthy conversation. 4 hours have passed I have talked with everyone but not with her because I don't know what to talk. Party got over and we went back home. Everyone had a great time. But I don't know my crush on her became a one sided love. After that whenevener I sleep she came into my dreams. it was the first experience for me. i am not feeling normal.

Days passed but that dreams won't stopped.

I talk this with one of my brother he had done the mastery of love and romance. I met him randomly. I told him my problem. He said talk with her start with making her as a friend. Go talk about it and firstly say sorry to her because you have hurted her. If you were in her place and she do this with you then what will you feel. I realised my mistake and was guilty. I just wanted to say sorry to her. i know I can't say her sorry face to face.

On my birthday i throw a party in which some of my friends came and one of them was my friends friend, He was studying in the same school where she was studying. I asked my friend to gather information about her. He had seen her many times but not knows her name. Then he phoned anyone and asked her name. Her official name is "Aditi". Till then i know her house name, Real struggle had started. I wanted any of her id to say her sorry. I know she was on Snapchat. I searched her but not sure what was his id. i messaged many girls and asked are you from this city. But none of them were.

22 April there was death anniversary organised of my loving grandpa. Everyone was invited. She had came too at night. My mother's too know that I wanted to talk with her. I guessed she too know her son has fallen in love with her.

Mom - He had been wanted to talk with you from long time.

Radhika - Ohh really aunty

I - Yes

(saying this I touched her mother's feet). And gave her indication to come with me. She followed me .Her mother went back with my mom there is only two of us in the room. We talked almost about everything. I made some of the jokes which made her laugh. Her mother too came and laughed on my jokes. One of my little cousin sister called her my spouse.

i got mini heart attack and watched her face the she too got shock then I changed the topic and silently signal all of the cousins to take her away she is a ransom.

Then we had dinner together. Some of my relatives seen me with her together they started talking with each other slowly like who's that adorable girl? They both looks nice together. Some of them even talked about our marriage.

Thank god she hadn't heard. While she was going I have asked my younger brother question about pie

because he is disturbing me and interrupting our conversation. But he was not able to tell. So she tooked his side and called me You are too boring and not like me bla bla bla but that boring word hurt me a lot. I started listening some of the sad songs too.

My love towards her convienced me to side my self respect and talk to her again. After some days there is the annversary of one of my father's closed friend in which she too had come. But I haven;t talked to her that time because of her words my mental states is not right at that time.

After some days of this incident on 9th may my father organised a party again.

She along with her sister were sitting on the drawing room. My mother asked me to talk and provide her my company. I forget everything and sat in front of the sofa on another sofa. Then we started conversation she was using her phone. I thought she don't like to talk with me but during the converstion she said "I have a podcast channel we are the team of 40".

I began asking questions related to her podcast channel like targeted audience, graphic designer, writer, voice editor, her role etc. Then I told her about my dream that I too wished to do a startup and start a podcast channel. Her tone got changed.

She : Nobody will work with you.

Me : Why?

She : Because you are new.

Why anybody should work with you?

Me : I can even pay them.

She again said bla bla bla bla

Me : It's upto you . You have time join my podcast or else I gonna will acquire your podcast one day.

(The reality was that all her team members are working for free her podcast had touched 6 million views but none of them got paid. All the money were taken by founders.)

I went into my room and made my podcast logo. Showing her I said I will surely compete you. My podcast channel name is REAL STORIES easily available on spotify.

This thing hurt me a lot i am so consious about my startup. She was my one sided love that's why i didn't said her anything. Now I have totally decided to compete her.

Once i started uploading episodes I got a message on whatsapp regarding the podcasts that i have copied her podcast.But my podcast and her differs a lo. If this incident doesn't happen with me then I surely save her name very different. But her words not only broke my heart. But also me her name is unknown in my contact.

One incident comes in my when ever I think about her one fine day when my father visits her house. She told him that she had been planned to take admission in Dehradun and also submitted the token money, When he come back home he scold me a lot by saying "You don't have any future tension". He scolds me continuously for

30 minutes.

After that I started filling a form in the same univesity where she was going. All the things were done only admission form fees is remaining. I too is enrolling on the same course in which she had enrolled. But, all his anger got lost. When I told him the course which I wanted to do was not in the list. No university or college had launched it's admission form for that course.

When she came I told her that "Buddy after hearing you have taken admission my father was scolding me".

We were laughing that time. Then I asked what's your plan are you surely moving to Dehradun.

Her reply was quiet shocking "Umm No ! I had taken back the admission fees. I am thinking of Delhi now.

Me : Why ? What happened ? Why had you changed the plan suddenly ?

She : Umm because that college was outside the city. I want to take some coachings too.

Now the people who are thinking she a studious girl. You all are wrong. This excuse is for parents. When I asked more about it she told " Buddy ! Delhi has more clubs. Night life of Delhi is awesome. There are also many reasons to move Delhi.

In short she wanted to enjoy her college life. I don't think there is anything wrong with this.

Me : Are you going alone?

She : Nope one of my close friend whom I meet in class 11 is coming with me too. Her name is Yena.

She showed me her pics. The surprising moment is that I know Yena from LKG. He has an elder brother his name is Amit. He is my friend.

After some day, when Amit and I met it's ordinary every almost month we meet. Since he was one of my good friend I asked him about it. She confirmed that Yena might will go. When I asked about Radhika. He knows her very well because they both are from the same school and his sister is her best friend. So almost every week she visits Yena house atleast 2 times.

He asked me how you know about her. I told him the story. His opinions are not right for Rudrika. May be she is too friendly or rude that's why people's are making rumors against her. This is one of the main problem of the society if a girl has a male friend. Then almost everytimes she will be judged by the society.

Sometimes I have seen that when a girl rejects a proposal then some of the boys just for the sake of their ego. They distribute her number on social media platforms or public places. Else they start making a rumor that she is characterless but all the things they say are totally baseless.

If any of the girl faces this problem. Then please file a cyber complaint don't be afraid. Tell this to your parents without hesitation. They are you parents they will always support you.

I don't know it was love or something different but her words hurted me like a needle. May be it was a just piece of attraction. After 20 days I have seen her, on my way towards my home in the morning. But this time i just feel better to ignore her and looked the other way. Self respect is also important.